Charlie!
Since the first day
I met you, I've always
thought you were special.
Best of Luck with the new
baby & God bless

Love,
Almost Famous
Rosalind

For Peggy and Korey

Look past the words, and feel the emotions

© Copyright 2005 Rosalind L. Jackson.
All rights reserved. No part of this publication may be reproduced, stored in a retrieval system, or transmitted, in any form or by any means, electronic, mechanical, photocopying, recording, or otherwise, without the written prior permission of the author.

Note for Librarians: A cataloguing record for this book is available from Library and Archives Canada at www.collectionscanada.ca/amicus/index-e.html
ISBN 1-4120-5111-8

Printed in Victoria, BC, Canada. Printed on paper with minimum 30% recycled fibre. Trafford's print shop runs on "green energy" from solar, wind and other environmentally-friendly power sources.

TRAFFORD

Offices in Canada, USA, Ireland and UK
This book was published on-demand in cooperation with Trafford Publishing. On-demand publishing is a unique process and service of making a book available for retail sale to the public taking advantage of on-demand manufacturing and Internet marketing. On-demand publishing includes promotions, retail sales, manufacturing, order fulfilment, accounting and collecting royalties on behalf of the author.

Book sales for North America and international:
Trafford Publishing, 6E–2333 Government St.,
Victoria, BC v8т 4р4 CANADA
phone 250 383 6864 (toll-free 1 888 232 4444)
fax 250 383 6804; email to orders@trafford.com
Book sales in Europe:
Trafford Publishing (uk) Ltd., Enterprise House, Wistaston Road Business Centre,
Wistaston Road, Crewe, Cheshire cw2 7rp UNITED KINGDOM
phone 01270 251 396 (local rate 0845 230 9601)
facsimile 01270 254 983; orders.uk@trafford.com
Order online at:
trafford.com/05-0006

10 9 8 7 6 5 4 3 2

Table of Contents

Poems in italics written between 1993 - 1997

Moment Of Clarity
It's Me
Undeniably Me
Do Me
What I Want
Insecure
Catch A Sale
Black Queen
Set Myself Free

Hate

Sold Your Soul
What Up " D "
Quit It
Broken Promise
Haters
Poem Cry
Commitment
Quit It Again
Hate Me Now
Five AM
Sacrifice
Loser
Question
Voice Mail
Damn
I'm Not Company

Opening Act

While sitting here,
Putting this book together.
I realized my life is much better.
I just put my soul on paper,
And I'm excited to see what happens later.
"Jay-Z, " answered all my questions.
I was afraid of failure,
So success never happened.
I know I use to be a mess.
I had issues stacked,
Next after next.
I knew therapy would be best.
And,
Acknowledging GOD,
Would deem me blessed.
I'm so in love with me,
Forgot about the insecure girl,
I use to be.
The beautiful woman I've grown to be,
Is the beautiful woman that was hidden inside of me.
Now,
I'm trying to write myself into history,
Creflo Dollar said,
Anointment of wealth was my Destiny.
Writing this book was a long shot,
But,
Just like everyone else I wanted to hit the jackpot.
I don't have the poor sob stories.

I'm not getting married until after I'm forty.
I've found self-discipline,
I've found my spiritual self-deep within,
So,
Turn the page and see where I've been.

May 18th, 2005

Wow, I still can't believe I'm actually publishing my poems. Every one has situations they must over come in life; however, I felt like I had been dealt an extra helping of truth, lies and deception. I was born in Frankfurt Germany, and living in Germany was one of the best experiences in my life. My parents wanted to make sure we experienced Europe, so we traveled by car, boat, bus, and foot to a lot of cities. My favorite was Italy.

Lately I've started to remember a lot more things about my childhood. I was an ambitious outgoing child; any opportunity I got to perform for people, I did. Living on a military base there wasn't many things to do, but I remember they had these talents shows called " Getting On the Hits." You picked a popular song, and lip-synced to an audience of 25 military families. Not to mention, cheerleading for the army base little league team, gymnastics, karate and there are so many more good memories.

So the question is: where did I go wrong; what caused me to make bad decisions and get inside my own head? It all started with an abusive relationship in college, intertwined with several bad memories of my childhood. Sometimes, I wonder how I even finished college. I even joined an organization because my insecurities made me feel that if I had those letters it would make me happier. I was wrong.

Issues, I had issues, so many issues. Then I met this guy, who cared enough to tell me I needed to seek professional help, so I did. My therapist, Mary-Alice Hines, started me on my road to recovery. It was nice to have an answer to why I did certain behaviors, and how I needed to overcome them. I was diagnosed as a co-dependent personality, and I suffered from ADHD. The first thing I did was to accept that there was something wrong with me.. Then, I started to slowly change my thought process and evaluating things before I re-acted. I even started to change everyday behavior around the house. I went from being messy, to an obsessed neat freak. You will never catch my bed unmade, unless I just woke up from an afternoon nap. I even say my eating habits changed. I put down the ast food and started eating from the USDA food pyramid. My biggest accomplishment, was overcoming my suppressed anger issues that I didn't even know I had. Instead of getting angry and lashing out, I put my feelings on paper. Most of all, I gained control over my emotions and that has been the most beneficial part of my growth. I started to love my dark skin, my thick body, my nappy hair, my big nose, and myself. My thought process has changed so much that my friend Josh excuses me of thinking like a man. Recently I came in contact with two college ex-boyfriends, and the only thing I thought to myself was, " How in the hell did I let these lames run games on me! "

When I was in college, I use to write poems for other people to use in their poetry class. I never saw it as being a gift and I was so lame that I did it for free. But, once again this guy helped me to realize that poetry was my gift. He encouraged me to write more, and dream big. I became a debt collector in 1997 and that is when I really started writing songs, short stories and poems. My first so-called book was " Broken Woman, Poems of Codependency." Then I wrote " From Caterpillar to Butterfly: Poems of Codependency to Independence." It was an extended adaptation of the first book. The more I got in touch with my environment, my feelings, and myself, I kept writing.

In 2000, I started to work for one of two mobile home debt collections agencies. This was the start of a slow slide backward, then a fast move forward. The first was the worst job in the world but the money was good. However, how much mandatory over time can anyone do before she realizes she didn't have a life anymore? The other company was an easy job, but it was one long bad episode of canceled sitcom. However, this company gave everyone stock in the corporation. When the company finally sold in December 2004, I took my money, put my faith in God's hand, and bailed!

Undeniably Me, represents my feelings and growth for the last ten years. During this time, I also fell head over heels for that one particular guy who helped me. All I can say is, he took me emotionally around the block and back. He's still a great guy and because of those trips he helped my mind heal even more. I think God places people and certain obstacles in your way for a reason. Some of the poems may seem like I am co-dependent but that is far from the truth. Our chemistry is undeniable and for some reason we can't get enough of each other.

This book is about my strength, learning to love my fellow man and learning to love myself. Most of all, I found a love for the Lord. When I finally let God into my life, I saw the world much clearer. Undeniably Me is forever changing, because even while I'm trying to put it together life is still going on. I wanted to take out the derogatory words and some poems that I wrote when people pissed me off. Yet, as an artist I can't compromise my art. If I offend anyone, oh well, get over it because life is too short. This was my learning process and my dream finally coming true. Most of all, I finally feel like my life has just begun. Enjoy.

Rosalind

Love

Love

Love

Love

Love

Love

Love

For Peggy

I feel your presence everyday.
You helped me to accept,
It was your time to go away.
I'm thankful,
God gave us that last day.
Korey, Bethel and six flags,
Would be the last time,
"I love you," your breath would say.
I took you for granted,
When you were alive.
I would've never taken you for granted.
If I could have sensed your demise.
You believed in my ability to write,
You're the reason,
My dream is finally coming alive.
You're the reason, I let God into my life.
You and God are the reason.
I'm happy for the first time.
And my love for the both of you,
Will last longer then,
Your lifetime.

Lost In Love

I'm lost in love,
A feeling from above,
So righteous,
It could only be God's love.
Only he can judge me.
He sees my heart sing,
And only wants good for me.
Showed me how good,
His love could be.
He represents,
The Love surrounding me.
He placed his blessings on me,
The path he wants for me.
The happiness his light,
Has promised me.
He is expanding my territory.
How did I live without he.
It's so much better,
Now he's with me.
I accept his love,
Graciously.
Living the rest of my life,
In harmony.
I'm lost in love,
The lord has show me.

Shown

Alone

Your hand caresses my thighs.
Stroking them so sensuously.
I feel the warmth of your breath,
On my navel,
While your lips glide gently past.
As you make your way,
Your tongue takes a ride,
Across my breast.
The sweet smell of baby oil,
On your breath,
Reminds me of the place,
You just left.
I wrap my fingers,
Around your neck,
And glide your lips against mine,
Getting my body prepared,
For that all night ride.
I opened my eyes,
And caught a glimpse,
Of the candlelight.
I listen to the Air,
And,
Notice an absent tone.
That's when I realized.
I was all,
Alone.

Beautiful Me

Beautiful Me,
Equally on the inside.
Screaming Taurus,
Do or die.
Only materialistic,
When it comes to me.
As for everyone else,
I just let them be.
Finally loving,
The color of my skin.
A,
Chocolate diva lived within.
My only issue is my job.
I'm tired of,
The corporate fraud.
It's time I free my soul,
I will no longer,
Be attached to a time clocks hold.
Not mention,
Debt collecting is getting old.
I need a new challenge,
In my life,
Plus all this drama is becoming trife.
Right now,
I'm in a zone.
No more sitting by a monitored phone.
I'm about to make,
West Peachtree my business.

I'd rather wait tables,
And,
Not have everyone in my business.
Oh beautiful me,
Corporate life isn't where,
I'm suppose to be.
It's time to seek my true,
Destiny.

Love At First Sight

At first, your physical beauty took me.
But after speaking to you,
Your words are even more beautiful.
I can close my eyes,
And pretend you're in my arms.
My heart beats strong.
With Admiration.
Your soft spoken words,
Brings a smile to my face.
The gentleness of your touch,
And the scent of your body,
Reassures me,
That my dream has come true,
But what good is a dram, *Dream*
Unless it becomes you.

Fate

Do you believe in fate?
From the moment I saw you,
I wanted to know your name, number,
And anything else.
You must think I'm crazy for writing this note.
But my emotions are too strong to hold.
Girlfriend yes? Girlfriend no?
What ever the answer may be,
I wanted to meet those pretty green eyes.
It is ever so seldom that I approach a man.
However,
When a smile is as exquisite as your smile.
It is only my duty to tell you,
How beautiful your smile shows.
Hello.

Undeniably Me

Da Girls

"D.C.,"
We were barley legal,
Meeting on the high school track.
17 years later,
You're the only one whose got my back.
You're the last connection,
To my craziness.
But,
I can't get rid of someone,
With whom I've been blessed.
"West Coast connection,"
You're going to be ok..
I keep you in my prayers,
Everyday.
So few people are as cool.
I keep good people near,
And you know that's one of Daddy's rules.
"Meeka,"
Let's order,
Another round of drinks,
So pass the drough,
And toast to Apple Martini's.
"Brooklyn,"
Why are you wasting your life?
Alabama is a dreamer,
And so should be his wife.
You're beautiful inside and out.
With that "Brook-Nam" history,

You'll succeed, no doubt.
Last but not least,
The Beautiful "Ms. Day,"
Encouraging me,
To put my poetry on display.
You're the type of friend,
I can holla at every couple of months,
I can't forget to thank you,
So you're the last name,
I put in quotes and fonts.

Love

At this very moment,
I realized that I didn't want to be your friend.
We shared a lot of good times,
Many memories that can't be forgot.
You were even around,
When another broke my heart.
Some day's you gave me a place to rest.
You even put my feelings to a test.
Then one day.
Something changed.
All of my feelings,
Were re-arranged.
It was a simple kiss on the cheek,
That led us both to seek.
The wild passion of the night.
Making love felt so right.
Yet,
We continued to be friends.
Hanging out now and then.
Some nights,
I slipped quietly in your bed.
And left early,
So nothing would be misled.
But now,
I can't be your friend.
One day,
I wanted you near,
But you couldn't be here.

I sat dazed and confused,
Not knowing what to do.
My stomach began to ache,
The pain in my head wouldn't go away.
The pounding of my heart was loud.
Each face looked like yours,
In the crowd.
That's why I can no longer be your friend.
I love you so much,
I want you to be my man.

Ecstacy

Songs of pleasure,
The sweetest melody.
A song played for you and me,
Of sweet ecstasy.
Your sweetest fantasy,
Of sheer harmony.
When I sing my song,
Each time you pleasure me,
Not one or twice,
But,
The magic of five plus three.
My body plays a song,
Of true ecstasy.

Moon

Look at the Moon,
And tell me what you see.
Could it be the reflection,
Of you and me?
Late in the evening,
When the moon start to rise,
Is the start of a sensual night.
Early in the morning,
When the moon starts to fade,
Reminds me of the beautiful love,
We just made.
The most beautiful moment,
Is when the moon is high in the sky,
Beyond everyone's reach,
As I release,
My natural high.

Emotionally Drained

You've got me emotionally drained.
I can' take another year
Of the same old games.
I never tripped on,
The way you hustle for dough.
Because what we had,
Was much larger than that glow.
Now,
Six years of this shit has gotten old.
You know I won't stand in the way.
I just don't want,
Six more months of checking in.
I don't want to think about,
Where your hands had been.
So Daddy,
I got to blow like the wind.
The only call I'm expecting,
Is when you say,
"Ma" this hustle is coming to an end.
Maybe then,
I'll go back to playing my position.
But right now,
My life is on a different mission.
I'd rather leave,
And let you handle your business.
I just refuse another day,
Of being emotionally missing.

That Day

That day I thought the world was about to end.
First Slick called,
And by the tone of his voice,
I knew it was about to begin.
I can hear Roy's words,
Ringing as loud as the liberty bell.
The story of your death,
Was told like a fairy tale.
I wept all night in Slick's arms.
I had never seen him cry,
Until you were gone.
I thank God he gave us Saturday.
I wish I knew,
It was going to be the last time,
I saw your face.
I would have spent more time.
I would have never left your side.
I would have kissed you on the cheek.
Sometimes I close my eyes,
And wish it was all a dream.
September 18th was the day you went home.
That will always be the day,
I was left alone.

Vee

There are so many things I could say,
But nothing will take the pain away.
When "Cali" broke me the news,
I suddenly fell to my knees,
And my tears flowed free.
Although,
I've only met Toya once,
Right now,
Thanksgiving is hunting my thoughts.
I loved her prissy attitude.
She was going to be as beautiful as you.
She's always standing right next to you.
May God bless Crystal,
And your family too.
Because he doesn't make any mistakes,
Just say good-bye for me,
At her wake.

Undeniably Me

Untitled

I can't get this man, out of my mind.
He's specifically one of a kind.
I never knew love could be so blind.
That yellow skin I can't deny.
When he's away,
I can't wait to see his face.
Brown eye's perfectly laced.
Not a hair out of place.
Wanda didn't make any mistakes.
When I'm alone,
I feel his soul, next to my bones.
The thought of him makes me moan.
Daddy, won't you please come home.
I know you feel this "Love Jones."
Or else, you would stay gone.
Can't nobody hit as deep in there.
You make my cherry scream, I swear.
Can't you taste I really care,
I'll swallow your life,
No need to dare.
Sometimes, I wonder if I'm making a mistake.
You said my heart you would never break.
Nevertheless, you make my heart ache.
In the end, I'll leave it to fate.
Every date, feels like our first date.
You're the only man, I can't hate.
You've never given me a reason to reciprocate.
Thank you for all the laughs,

The comfort when Peggy passed.
I'm glad I met your high yellow ass.
You've made her baby girl, world class.
I just live day to day.
I can't fathom the thought,
Of you going away.
Our friendship is here to stay.
We'll always be Taurus's
The 6th and 9th of May

Tomato Soup

One can of Tomato Soup,
Sent my heart falling in love with you.
I know we've been through so much.
And,
I have a tendency to keep my guard up.
We had a good time at follies,
Until that stripper didn't realize,
I was your Mommy.
Then your Boy,
Was asking me for shit in two's.
Between that stripper and him,
I didn't know what to do.
I started feeling sick
Too many pills and drinks don't mix
Then the night ended,
With tomato soup,
Deja vu,
A big black bucket,
And,
Lazarus feelings Mommy's blues.
It was one of those days,
I kept wishing would go away.
Until
The tomato soup,
And falling asleep,
Next to you

Mental

Without saying a word,
We gaze into each other's eyes,
And read each other's minds.
Our eyes are our path to righteousness.
Our path to completeness.
Our path to the other's inner thoughts.
Please don't look away.
Please don't be afraid,
Please don't be scared.
To find our mental connection.
It is the key to lead us,
On our path together.
Together our eyes,
Will look for the same.
It's not necessary to blink.
You will miss my heart,
The brief second you look away.

Jealousy

Do we even compare?
When you're with me, do you have thought's of her?
Do I have to worry, each time you leave my door?
When we're not together, who is on your mind?
When you're looking for love, whom do you choose to spend,
Your time?
Am I jealous?
You're damn right I am.
Why do I have to share the person,
I want to call my man.
Why must I feel insecure, night after night?
I no longer find it necessary,
To continue this fight.
You don't have to choose me.
Because I'm letting myself go.
Jealousy no longer
Hangs at my door

Foam Bath

Do you remember our Foam Bath?
Except,
We didn't have any water,
Just a rag.
Then you broke out the scented oil.
It wasn't brand new,
But I know you're still loyal.
I laid below your stomach.
And,
The way you played with my ears,
I knew you were loving it.
You dropped to your knees,
Pulled me close with a squeeze.
Our bodies were in-sync.
Our minds were the second link.
Even Lazarus took a peek.
You softly whispered in my ear,
"Don't you know, Daddy's always here?"
Now when I take a foam bath,
I "reminisce" of no water,
Just Lazarus, Daddy,
And a rag.

Dangerously In Love

I'm dangerously in Love with you .
But,
I prayed to God to harden my heart.
Cause when I can't see you,
It tears me apart.
He still hasn't granted my wish,
Why else would I be writing this?
I play it cool when you come around.
All I think about is how to lay you down.
I can't show how I feel around you.
Because every heartbeat,
Is so dangerously true.
You're out to conquer the world.
And it ain't about being called your girl
I understand the profession you choose.
It's only the "hustle,"
That makes my heart bruise.
I hear the slick shit you say on the low.
Baby you make it so hard for me to go.
I can hear it in your voice.
The way you say my name.
I can see it in your eyes,
Pretty browns feeling my pain.
You came through one special day.
Now,
My girls understand why I feel this way.
Except when it's girls night on the town.
They're searching for some cuties.

While I sit back,
And enjoy a black and mild.
Nigga's can't understand,
Why I make them step.
I'm not the type of girl, who settles for less.
I roll home alone each night.
Because,
I'm finally contempt with my life.
Sometimes I get lonely for you.
But I accept,
You got to do, what you got to do.
Besides, these feelings just won't die.
I'm dangerously in love,
And I don't know why,

Me

Me

Me

Me

Me

Me

Me

Royal Blessings

I'm seeking my royal blessing,
Me and Laz,
Popping bubbly and sharing affections.
Wearing all the latest collections,
Oprah calling with financial lessons.
I want to dance in St. Tropez,
Waving at "Hov" and "B" across the way.
Only Dayton Nigga's up in the place,
Then off to Amsterdam to smoke some hay.
I'll can finally afford my Birkin bag.
Manolo Blahnik shoes, and Harry Winston jewels.
The only girl that has ever been true.
"D.C." you know I got you.
I can't forget Daddy,
Who brought out the writer in me,
Another day of work,
he will never see.
I'll buy Roy a Navigator truck,
So he can spend his last years,
fishing and living it up.
I would grant Korey his every dream,
Send him to Harvard because,
Of the potential I see.
I'll move Peggy within my reach,
And drop her name,
On lifestyles with Robin Leech.
Only I can make this dream come true,
With royal blessings,
From you know who.

A Star Left Behind

I was a star denied her destiny.
When my mind was weak,
I'd let others get the best of me.
Then I dreamt,
I was shot in the throat.
Daddy's karma.
Left a real big hole.
I dropped to my knees,
And the Lords Prayer spilled out.
I stood up grabbed the hole,
God let me know it wasn't my time to go.
I even got to accuser-her.
No chicken is standing in the way,
Of my future,
I opened my eye's
As I gasped one last breath,
And happy it was only a dream,
Disguised as a test.
I thank God for my stock option,
It left me with only one option.
I quit my job,
And stepped out on faith,
Leaving behind the skeptics,
Of that hatred pace.
It's time everyone see,
What I've been denied.
With the strength of God and my mind,
I will no longer be a star,
Left behind.

Truth, Lies And Deception

I,
Lie to you,
To get what I want,
Truth is something,
That can't be sought.
Deception,
Is the words,
I live by.
I know you love me,
So,
There is no need to cry.
My world,
Is full of complicated lies.
Telling the truth,
Makes it harder to server ties.
I never meant to hurt you,
But my life,
Is one big disguise.
So crying over me,
Is a waste of time.
Maybe it's time,
You face the facts.
I love you,
And that's no lie.
I got to be free,
And that's the truth.
I'm sorry,
For deceiving you.
But,

It's all about me
And not about you.

Moment Of Clarity

I can finally say I'm ok,
And life is much better this way.
I thought I was issue free,
But my mom's death,
Was holding me.
It was her spirit that led me home.
Thanksgiving,
Shouldn't be spent alone.
My father looked great.
I guess he's happy,
With his new mate.
I'll give her pass,
Since she can fix a plate.
But,
If she fucks over Roy,
I'm going to seal her fate.
Then I had to go see my mom,
It had been way too long.
When I kneeled by her grave,
I found the moment of clarity,
That I craved.
My soul sighed in relief.
My mind felt at peace,
God's my new belief,
I no longer carry,
My mother's grief.

Undeniably Me

It's Me

What ya, looking for,
You haven't found in the past.
Someone to make it last,
No other Nigga can have.
A dream girl for life,
Just to be you wife,
But the search continues,
Many hoes on the menu.
Close your eyes,
And wish upon a star,
The woman that you seek,
Is a friend in your heart.
She stands before you.
Always adored you.
Never could ignore you,
Hoped good for you.
She played her position,
Not on a mission.
If a Nigga stepped to her,
Nothing but dis'ed him.
She's down for life.
You know she would even fight.
Take a hit or two,
Roll a blunt for you.
No need for inspection,
She's molded to perfection.
Why settle for less when,
You had the best hen.

When she's by your side,
Money flowed nice,
Even helped put you on,
Through the bad times.
You enjoyed the ride.
She's nothing to be played with,
A masterpiece created.
A friend for life,
That could have been your wife.
But the search continues,
Many hoes on the menu.

Undeniably Me

I'm "Undeniably Me,"
One of God's blessed child's,
So do I dare to make my dreams go wild.
Or do I choose to sit back and lose.
Just another sister,
Screaming the white man blues.
No, not this time,
I put my past behind.
Something much stronger is guiding me.
He's my agent with no fee.
And,
He got my Momma by his side,
Making sure baby girl comes out all right.
I finally know who I be.
Pretty Chocolate,
And,
A little bit sexy.
The Parisian type of girl.
Never needed those "20 Pearls."
Daddy blessed me with my first Kenneth Cole,
Now each day my gear just flows.
But the real women you still don't know.
I'm only material when it comes to me,
I accept anyone for who they be.
All I know,
Is that I'm undeniably me.
And I'm choosing,
My own Destiny.

Do Me

I'm suppose to be,
Just doing me.
Fulfilling my dreams.
Making lots of cram,
Mercedes my whip.
Crib by Phipps,
I'm going to have,
All of this.
Thinking of myself.
Forget everyone else,
Freedoms strapped,
Right under my belt.
I'll buy my parents,
A house by the beach.
Let them retire comfortably,
A small price to pay,
For raising my seed.
I'm a chocolate Godiva.
Independent survivor.
God's my messiah,
Watch my dreams,
Transpire.
My secret is unique,
I'll just do me

What I Want

I want,
To wake up around ten.
Buttering croissants,
While my Gevalia is brewing.
Meet my personal trainer downstairs,
To put this body in complete repair.
After noon,
I'll start to handle my business,
Making moves,
Because I want my ends endless.
Apple Martini's after five,
To set the evening off right.
I'll inhale in the early evenings
And exhale whatever pleases me.
I'll toast all through the night.
Thanking God,
For my ability to write.
When the party's over,
And my mind is clearer.
I'll meet up with "Daddy,"
For some naked twister.
Right before I fall asleep,
I'll thank the Lord,
For blessing me.

Undeniably Me

I'm Not Insecure

I'm not insecure.
That's the one thing,
I refuse to be.
Trapped inside of me.
Not knowing whom to believe.
Missing out on the world.
Didn't know,
I was a beautiful girl.
Insecure,
Is what I use to be.
But,
That chick is dead to me.
Dark, Chocolate, Brown.
Those names,
Sound sweet to me now.
I'm as real as I can be,
My insides,
Are as beautiful as me.
I'm,
A diamond with clarity.
A sister,
With no insecurities.
There's no need,
To worry about me,
Because insecure,
Is what I refuse to be.

Catch A Sale

Call me catch a sale queen.
For some reason sales just find me.
Michael Kors, Nicole Miller and DJP's
They all make my feet sing.
At the concert.
It was Beyonce, Prada, and me.
Coach hat, Coach purse, Coach shoes,
And they all match perfectly.
Floor length DKNY wool skirt,
I'm building a wardrobe,
I never have to give up.
Some of ya'll are saying,
"I got her on some things"
At least I'm living within my means,
And still stepping so fresh and so clean.
It's more than about catching a sale.
I bought my first Coach when I was thirty,
I never faked it,
Because that made me feel dirty.
I could've bought the little purse everyone carries,
But I'm not everyone,
And being basic isn't necessary.
And,
My purses are all low-key,
I didn't receive a check,
For rocking those damn C's!
Your black Express pants are really cute.
But,

I prefer my $200.00 Laundry,
And I paid the same price as you.
There isn't anything wrong with,
Rave and Level 10.
But,
I'm building a collection,
"Phipps Plaza" is my selection,
And you can find me,
In the sale section

Black Queen

I'm seeing shade of gray,
My mind is filled with haze.
I dropped out of sight,
And lost points on a stupid fight.
Now,
I'm trying to regain my reign,
As your beautiful Black Queen.
Stepped up to the plate,
Admitted I was wrong.
Thankful you're still here,
Because you could be gone.
My mind started to think,
Of sweet love we made,
Sex games we played,
It all could have faded,
To past memories.
I would have been dreaming,
Of you and me.
Right now I'm pleased,
You gave me this chance to freeze.
This moment in time,
My thoughts are on rewind.
I'll be your righteous one,
Trying to make you happy.
You always be my daddy,
My love is blind like justice,
No death sentence can bust us,
Apart you're my heart,

And today I make my mark.
Forever I will reign
As your Beautiful Black Queen.

Set Myself Free

It's time I set myself "Free."
I've got to stop these,
"Bad Habits,"
Between you and me.
I've changed your ring tone,
To "Through with Love."
Because,
"I've changed my mind,"
And exhaled all the dreams you spoke of.
"Ma I promise, it's just you and me!"
But those figures,
Keep adding to three,
And,
Your drama is spilling over to me.
You can't imagine,
The sorrow and perplexities,
You put me through.
Maybe that is the reason,
Jason and Randy,
Are partying in your dreams.
Because,
You only value material things.
And I'm the one piece of material,
You can't keep.
Now,
It's time I break your heart.
You got your situation to ease your fall.
Go ahead and cry on her shoulder,

Because I'm setting myself "Free."
From,
This "Emotional Roller Coaster."

Hate

Hate

Hate

Hate

Hate

Hate

Hate

Sold Your Soul

You once told me your boy sold his soul,
For a business and a dream.
He'd never know what love means,
Because his wedding ring,
Didn't mean a thing.
You missed one important fact.
You can sell your soul,
In more ways than that.
Daddy,
I know you were going to get right back,
But,
Baby Girl, deserves much better than that.
Now my mind is extra tight.
I'm not playing foolish another night.
You told me I was the female version of you.
I would've played the game the same way too.
However,
I'm not into playing games.
Right now abstinence is my thing.
Shaking off these feelings is my middle name.
Yet,
How do I walk away from love?
I heard all the dreams you spoke of.
I'm the girl you wanted to spend the rest of your life.
Can't count the times you said I'll be your wife.
Play on Player,
I ain't made you're doing your thing.
Take them hoes for all their cream.

See,
You don't have to marry someone to sell your soul.
Neglecting the one you love,
Is still the devils hold.

What up "D"

What up "D",
I can't figure you out.
You got more issues,
Than this Nigga can count.
Somehow you got it confused.
And,
Thought a smoke break meant we were cool.
Since I put those Black and Milds down.
Your silly little ass started wilding out.
I never met a man as messy as you.
If I didn't have a life,
I guess I would be messy too.
Think about all the trouble you keep.
Then you had the nerve to lie on me.
I told you in the office.
We would never be cool.
That means no need to be nice,
And play yourself for a fool.
Why are you always scratching your nuts?
"CVS" got something,
For that kind of stuff.
Your girl told me,
You were obsessed with me,
You ain't happy unless you're glimpsing at me.
Not only do I have the beauty,
But brains to match.
My real friends will tell you.
My soul is even better than that.

A Nigga from the streets helped mold me.
He taught me Nigga's like you,
Are obsolete.
I know a psychiatrist you can go to for free.
As long as your crazy ass,
Stay away from me.
You didn't even know I could get this deep.
That's why I'm shouting out,
"What up "D".

Quit-It

Quit-It,
The only thing bright about you is your skin.
Your old ass is rep'n, Chicken to the end.
I feel sorry for you,
These "Nigga's,"
Got you playing the fool.
So get over yourself,
Maybe God,
Will bless you,
With the cards you were dealt.
A year ago.
We were flying to Hawaii,
So you could marry that,
"20" something year old Hottie.
Next think I know.
Your doing a "B" & "E" at his crib.
That was right before the clinic,
Signed you in.
Two months later,
You moved on to your next victim.
Now,
You got his broke ass "acting" a fool.
You did clean him up,
That's kind' a cool.
Got him wearing Burberry,
No,
I meant "Furberry,"
With a Fresh new cut,

He's not a "Ken" doll
You can play dress up.
I should tell him,
What you say behind his back.
Why would you talk that loud?
Unless it was intended,
For me to here that.

hear

But,
I'd rather you stay six feet above.
You're the entertainment,
Poetry books are filled of.
I'd like to, wish you the best,
But if you don't stop
Minding my business.
You're going to hate,
What I say next............

Broken Promise

I will,
Not sit back and cry,
Over another broken promise,
You have made.
What good is a promise?
If your word can't be saved.
A promise is your word,
And you said,
Your word is bond.
but lately,
Your promises,
Keep singing,
That same old song.
Baby I'm sorry,
Baby I promise,
It won't happen anymore.
Your damn right,
Because your butt,
Is hitting the door.
I do promise,
To not let you,
Back into my life.
Or,
Give your sorry ass,
Another try.
Now it's your turn,
To sit back and cry,
Because my promise,
Is not a lie.

Haters

It must be hard in the trenches,
I hear when my name gets mentioned,
The hating starts commencing.
"Ms. Jackson don't work here no more."
"She ain't that good anyway."
You were at the awards ceremony,
For two years straight.
When they announced #1 on the team,
I had them saying my name.
And we opened the very same day!
This corporate shit ain't my Destiny.
But while I'm here,
I'm not letting it get the best on me.
It's all about that bonus,
My salary with a little extra on it.
Most of ya'll just come here to date,
Spending most of your time,
Fucking in the stairway.
Plus your salary,
Is the most money you've ever made.
And I know for a fact,
You ain't paid like I'm paid.
Compared to some other jobs,
This is damn near pocket change.
You heard the rumors about the downsize,
I bet you beat my black ass,
To the unemployment line.
I almost forget about that other lie.

How I was bragging about my status,
And couldn't be sacrificed.
See,
I'm just humble, beautiful and smart.
Don't you know Karma come back,
Much harder than it was sought.
That's why I continue,
To shake you haters off.

Undeniably Me

Poem Cry

You saw me.
But,
I saw your yellow ass,
Beaming right through.
Didn't you see me pause,
For a minute,
I wish you could have seen,
The humor in it.
It's not what you think.
Let's say,
My curiosity got the best of me.
And,
That's fucked up,
What you told "Foot's"
I though we kept out shit,
Between the two of us.
What if I told him about...
Nah.... but,
Let me hear some more of our stuff,
And,
I'm going to start spilling my guts.
Yet,
I thank "Foot's" for the love,
The same appreciation "A" thought of.
Even "D" gave me,
A thank you hug.
It's the small things,
Slicks not appreciative of.

I'm the queen of your chess game,
You want me to play my position,
Then,
You try to play me with those chickens.
I'll give you 5 seconds,
To think of what you're about to be missing.
Just because you say I'm your wife.
Am I suppose to be content
Being the future Mrs. Slick?
My heart is no longer in it.
That's why I'll let this poem cry.
Right before I disappear,
Out of your life.

Commitment

It's over?
Is that just a gesture?
Or,
A sign of weakness?
You're in denial,
At the thought of commitment.
Take a long look,
At what's ending.
You dam well know,
I'm not pretending.
It's over?
Are you sure?
I'm finished with the sorrow.
There was a time,
I would let you slide back tomorrow.
It's over?
You promise to God?
You're not joking right?
We are through tonight!
You're moving on from me,
And,
I'm not looking back at you.
Now are you sure?
Or,
Did the idea of Commitment,
Scare you?
I have nothing to confess,
Is that why our life is a mess?

It's the big "C",
Your fear of you and me.
No need to come back,
Or even ask why.
I'm committed no longer,
To living a lie!

Quit It Again

It's a shame we keep meeting like this.
I lied to "Brooklyn," when I said,
"Quit it" would be your last dis.
You're an insecure black woman.
Always yapping on the phone.
With a voice,
That sounds like a long dial tone.
I must admit,
I did fuck with you a bit.
I love that insecure shit.
I apologize for my entertainment,
At your expense.
But,
I kept plenty of your secrets.
Working under the code,
Mind your own business.
Yet I had to warn your,
Ex "not" finance's girl on the low,
I wasn't the first to let her know.
You were hating to the man for show.
You damn near turned white,
When you saw us together.
You didn't know if we were,
Plotting together,
Getting coffee together,
It sent you on an insecure endeavors.
Then,
You had the nerve,

To ask to speak to me in private.
Did you think I cut you off,
So you could some back and revive it?
Once again,
"Brooklyn", and me
Had a laugh compliments of you.
It's about time you get a clue.
The company offers free therapy,
For crazy people too.
I should spill your secrets.
Across this paper.
Piss me off again,
And I won't be responsible,
For what I write later.

Hate Me Now

What did I do to you?
To make you act like a fool.
We don't even speak,
And that's cool with me.
My girl gave me a warning,
Your the type of bitch,
That'll fuck up my morning.
See,
All that bullshit you brewed.
It's coming back to hunt you.
Karma hurts in the worst way
Especially for those that like to hate.
Why me?
Is it because,
I don't have to cheat to hit my goal?
Or Kiss some ass and be told no?
Maybe you're just envious of me?
I'm a rare commodity.
Pretty as can be,
Ask anyone that's real,
And they'll tell you,
I'm just as sweet.
I seen your awards stacked like a tree,
Where'd you get that?
Oh yea,
Me.
But you see,
I took mine down.

Those awards don't mean shit to me.
Working for whitey,
Seems to be your destiny.
Bowing down to whitey,
Is the affirmation you need.
Go ahead and take a bow,
Because your old ass,
Can hate me now.

Five A.M.

I loved you,
More than I loved myself.
I understand you're my friend.
Only in my mind,
You were my man.
I never thought,
I'd admit this.
I was a game,
You played with.
I only tried to be,
The support,
A brother needs.
I was down in your ball'n days
Alcohol,
Weed,
Too many parties.
Accepted your collect calls.
Was there,
When your attorney got you off.
I didn't dis you,
When your dough was low,
But now I wonder,
If I should have though.
It's five A.M.,
And I'm feeling lonely.
Back in the day,
I would have run,
To you right away.

Now,
That I'm changing my mind,
No more,
Sleepless nights.
No more,
Five A.M. writes.

Sacrifice

Why should I sacrifice,
My life?
To make you feel,
Like the man you are not.
I awake,
Work,
And slave,
To your needs.
Without,
A simple praise of me.
Do this, (slap)
Do that, (punch)
Do as I say,
Not as I do.
I don't think so,
My sacrificing,
Days are through.
So step aside,
You pitiful man,
And,
Watch my mind at ease.
Now,
You're on your own,
And will find yourself,
Begging me please.
Now,
Watch my long strides,
Walk straight out the door,

Because,
I never needed you,
You needed me,
Much more.
Sacrifice is over!

Undeniably Me

Loser

Fat boy D,
I've decided to rename you.
How many times can a loser really lose?
Other losers that crossed my path,
Hated once,
And felt my wrath.
But you are a loser or another kind.
You keep setting yourself up,
Now I got to hit your ass for a second time.
"L" is for you little mans complex,
It's obvious you lack more than good sex.
"O" is for the other,
Nigga's that don't fuck with you.
They re-named you,
"Fat Girl" fool!
"S" is for the sympathy I feel for you wife.
You have the symptoms,
To batter a poor girls life.
"E" is for the "extra" large size you should wear.
Stop wearing your son's clothes,
Cause they're riding up there.
"R" is for how you represent yourself each day,
Six diet Pepsi's, 12 cigarettes,
Sandals with socks,
Your "Apex" is losing its "x."
Your desk and your car,
Represent one cluttered mess.
I'm not trying to send you a hint.

But,
Renaming you "Loser,"
Is just a compliment.

Question?

Question?
Am I the girl you love?
Wasn't I the one you said you dreamed of?
Is your ego deeper than our love?
Is your balling all you think of?
Didn't I save your life?
Didn't I have you calling me your wife?
Didn't I have you stop fronting for your friends?
Didn't I have you claiming me until the end?
Doesn't the hustle rule your life?
Doesn't the hustle come before your wife?
Don't you just live to be in the game?
Don't you just love never taking the blame?
Don't you get tired of Hustling to eat?
Don't you get tired of hurting me?
Do you feel sorry for my secrets you didn't keep?
Do you feel sorry for the secrets I might leak?
Did you ever think, I would leave your life?
Did you every think, I wouldn't be your wife?
Did you ever think, I wouldn't be there?
Did you ever think, for you I don't care?
Did you ever think?
Question?

Voice Mail

I knew I had enough,
When I got that damn voicemail.
It was the last sign that told the tale.
Listen baby girl, it's time to bail.
I tried to hide the truth through and through.
But now,
My head is saying,
It's time for you to lose.
So for once I spoke my mind,
And sent you a message,
Bigger than any line.
You know you hurt me too,
Because I got your message,
And,
Player that's something we don't do.
I'm tired of all the games,
In the end,
Will you ever take the blame?
I want to thank you boo,
This woman was crafted,
Compliments of you.
Not the weak little girl you once used.
But a Chocolate Godiva,
Ever so smooth.
Listen baby boy,
It's time to bail.
Time to break free,
Of pretty Slick's jail.

It's all because of the damn voicemail.
The very last sign that told the tale.

Damn

A new chapter is about to begin,
I guess this book is never going to end.
So coming to the stage,
Is a skinny Nigga,
That loves to hate.
Damn,
You're turning this book,
Into a dedication,
So I have to ask,
Why do you love hating.
You would have never been a part,
Of the Dynasty,
"Brooklyn" and I created.
You wanted a piece of the big bonus club,
But your numbers kept,
Dissipating.
Remember the day,
I was in your face,
Giving you the chance,
To explain why you love to hate.
I can still hear you stuttering.
As if Scooby Doo was trying to escape.
I tried to be the "bigger" man.
After I showered your baby,
You had the audacity to hate again.
The money I was making,
Was the root of your evil,
You're a dark skinned weasel,

Now you're just another hater,
I've painted on my easel

I'm Not Company

What up "A"
Long time no see,
Since you've been away,
Company I ceased to be.
You thought I was a bird,
You thought I was gone,
Nigga's you didn't know,
This was "Slicks" plan all along.
He gave me a book and a pen,
With a set of instructions.
He gave me tough love.
Even tougher than I had growing up.
Didn't you see that change in me?
A pretty black girl,
Without all that weave.
I even caught you trying to hate,
Conversations about the "Acura",
You slipped in around eight.
You didn't know,
That "Acura" shit wasn't pure.
You didn't know,
I'm not the type of girl who's insecure.
You didn't know,
That I blessed that shit.
Now you know,
I was always down with it.
Then you asked me for some tongue,
Running game on me has long been done.

I loved the look on your face,
When "Daddy" confirmed my status
At his place.
When it comes to Company,
"A",
You'll win that race

Me

Me

Me

Me

Me

Me

Me

In Love With Me

I'm in love with me.
Chocolate as I want to be.
Nice and think in my anatomy,
Rocking gear with validity.
Lord please keep blessing me.
I'm no longer a poison pen.
I take a step back,
And count to ten.
Writing what I'm feeling.
Now,
My mind has finished healing.
Strictly about business dealings.
Dreaming of the silver screen.
By-lines in magazines,
Making all the hot scenes.
I'm no longer living quarantined.
Letting no man intervene.
It's time for celebration.
Self-love without aggravation.
Don't need anyone's affirmation,
Refusing their complications.
Either,
You can ride or take a vacation.
It's the world versus me,
Go ahead,
Hate every bit of me.
You'll never get rid of me.
For many I am the epitome.

But,
I only know,
That I'm in love with me.

I'm A Star

Since,
I was a seed,
I knew a star lived in me.
Somehow,
I got off my path,
And,
I'm ready to take my place at last.
If it wasn't for Daddy,
My life would be misplaced,
Even through the hurt,
He helped this star escape,
Paul made me realize,
My strength was always inside of me.
It just took me a little longer,
To reach my destiny.
So,
I'm scribbling my way,
Into history.
Only Mars,
Can shine brighter than me

Still Looking

Sitting here,
Drowning my tears,
Fears no longer wanted here.
Wanting to make a change,
Be the right way,
Flipping the script,
No time to play games,
Pretty face on,
Spitting lace thongs,
Hair's done,
But what is really going on?
Don't know.
Can't figure it out.
Why life's such a drought.
Yet,
I stay outfitted in new gear,
But my look can be mistook.
Take a look at my broken heart.
No words need to be spoken,
Looking for a token to slide right in,
And represent a real man.
Not looking for a handout,
I only make 40 a year.
But spending twice that.
Scheming, dealing, stealing and now healing.
Sitting in a window scribbling.
Truck rolling by, cars of the fly,
Birds trying to creep,

Mexicans painting the street,
While the sunshine blinds me.
My minds at ease, teased and pleased.
Wishing life was a breeze.
No more time to sweat the bad,
Time to start enjoying life and not the sad.
A new beginning starts today.
Making my life great.
It's my world now play.

Sense Of Self

My poem will blaze you,
Amaze you.
I'm make you join my organization,
Then I'll haze you,
With knowledge and a sense of self.
My oratory speaks for its self.
You're non-existent, offensive.
Institutionalized since an infant.
Let go your oppressor,
Be the aggressor,
Pledge to yourself,
That you will make your life better.
Take no labels,
Recant others fables,
You're being put on notice,
To get your life stable.
You're the epitome of God,
You personify his hue.
Never let a mortal disrespect you.
Knowledge is your narcotic.
Don't get caught without it.
Forget being bout it, bout it.
Recognize your reality.
Seize your morality,
And ignore the propaganda
Being fed to you and me.
Listen to my prophecy,
Make your life a priority.

Your prognosis is a self-esteem.
Become self sufficient,
And independent,
No other man,
Could ever f--- with it.

Undeniably Me

Natural High

I'm on a natural high.
The kind of high.
A dub can't buy.
The fiends could sweep,
The streets all night.
Still couldn't inject,
What I feel inside.
One snort,
Of the whitest snow,
Couldn't beat,
My natural blow.
"X" can make you,
Shake your pants.
Except my high,
Is saving the last dance.
Crack can leave you,
Poor and broke.
What I got,
Is wrapped in quotes.
Acid can have you,
Seeing things.
What I got
Is better than fake dreams.
"GHB" can render you,
Comatose.
My high,
Keeps me naturally afloat.
My high is about life,
Naturally blessed,
loved and bright!

It's You

Last night was a trying time.
I didn't know if I was in love with you,
Or just the image of you in my mind.
A man stepped to me, so kind and sweet.
I wanted it to be you, but it couldn't be.
He told me how beautiful,
And lovely I was.
He told me my skin,
Was as smooth as a chocolate dove.
The type of chocolate that is extremely sweet,
And much more expensive,
Than any plain Hershey.
It set my mind back for a moment.
Of memories that use to be.
How you once told me,
That you were happy to meet me.
You even told me,
How you loved the color of my skin.
I wish that was now,
But unfortunately,
That was back then.
Now standing before me,
Is a man full of gaze,
I'm trying to figure out.
How I got his mind in such a daze.
How is it,
This man stand before me,
With such radiant praise.

How is it,
He sees something you haven't seen in days.
Then I remembered,
The problem isn't with me.
It's you.

Best Of Me

Did you think?
You'd get the best of me?
This pretty, chocolate thing,
Got you changing the way you think.
I bet you never thought,
You'd lose me.
I see the way you look at me.
My peripheral vision,
Is as good as my ESP.
I hated having that dream,
It was something I didn't want to see.
Your game was about to change,
Once again,
You couldn't say my name.
I'm just another game,
Except you were playing for keeps.
And you forgot one thing,
None of my fingers,
Were rocking a ring.
Was I suppose to sit back,
And let you get the best of me.
Continue to let you play me,
Just like a chess piece.
Tell me how life feels,
Without me.
Because only I,
Can get the best of me.

1999 didn't happen.
No joke, my life was up in smoke.
Weed that's blessed from the God's,
Sent straight to my body.
Games played, relationships fade,
Now I sit here writing poems.
Trying to find what ~~with~~ wrong, with my life.
went I started out right.
Blessed from the heavens, sent to my parents.
Good Mom, Good Dad,
Never Hungry, Never Sad.
Gave love, Gave Gifts,
Every child's only wish.
But I had none of their sense.
Why did I flip like a broken arrow,
And not fly like a sparrow.
Because of love, love from whom,
Love from a man.
A love never found, they turned my life upside down.
I was barely getting by,
But still trying to live fly.
Still looking for love?
No,
My own sanity has me changing my mind.
I know what I got to do.
Create someone new.
I looked inside of my self,
And I found a love I never felt.

I fell in love with me,
And that's the only way it's going to be.
I may never have love for a man.
But I'll love myself,
The best way I can.
Now that I finally know,
My life is about to go.
Ahead where it's suppose to be.
Living in the lap of luxury.
Making my money, making my life right.
Fuck a man, because this is my life.
If he do come he better come right.
I'm through with the games,
And if he can't love me the same.
The same way I do,
He's through.
1999 this one was for you.

Tired Of Falling

I'm tired of falling,
In love with you.
Tired of playing the fool,
Tired of being lied to.
Tired of all the games,
Tired of taking the blame.
Tired of being without you.
Tired of guessing,
Who's with you.
Tired of the things you say,
It's just pillow talk anyway.
You want to have your cake,
And it eat it too.
I just tired of falling for you!

Free

I'm finally free.
No issues,
Holding me.
That fly type of girl,
Finally living life,
Like it's,
The end of the world.
Through asking for help.
That's not,
The cards I was dealt.
My fortune,
Has been told.
I'll receive all I behold,
My soul,
Has been released,
Destiny's within my reach,
I've got good people,
By my side.
Inspiring all that I write.
It's knowledge that I seek,
Forehead kisses,
And one on the cheek.
Looking forward,
To each day.
So that I can say,
I'm finally free,
No issues holding me.

Pretty Girl

What up "Pretty Girl,"
Your masculine voice portrays.
Those two little words,
Fill me with,
Sweet, secure and sensual praise.
Those two little words,
Got me feeling,
Like I smoked an ounce,
Of purple haze.
So,
I wrote this poem,
And went back to sleep.
Because you told me to,
And baby were just that deep.
Sometimes,
You're the sanest part of my day.
One "PG" from you,
Washes my blues away.
With you,
It ain't all about my looks.
I'm like your investment,
Written inside this undeniable book.
You've molded me,
Into the female version of you.
Then you stepped back,
And left the rest for me to do.
Bitches,
Gonna be sick,

When our last name,
Is reading the same.
But you know,
I don't need that ring.
That piece of paper,
Is just a political fiend.
All I need,
Is you across the street,
Reminding me,
Of,
The "pretty girl"
I grew to be.

Butterflies

Driving down 85,
Tears in my eyes,
Horns blowing.
But,
All I hear,
Is my heart pounding?
I wipe the tears away,
Pretend I'm O.K.
But every breath,
Wants to say your name.
My head aches.
My mind is playing games.
But by broken heart,
Is in more pain.
Can't you see,
What your doing to me.
At night I can't sleep.
Wishing the butterflies,
Would go away.
What do I do,
What do I say?
To make you understand,
I don't want to be this way.
I know I have issues,
But,
I thought you would stay.
Because of my insecurities,
You have gone away.

And,
The butterflies,
Are here to stay.

Cry Another Tear

Where do I go from here,
When love has me in tears.
Do I just run and hide,
Or express what I'm feeling inside.
I keep asking what happened to us,
Two people filled with love and trust.
I wonder if it all was a lie,
But true love you can't deny.
I remember the very first day,
You started keeping me away.
Then I slowly saw you change,
The way you looked, it was all explained.
At first it was cold brown eyes,
Then it changed to a hypnotize.
I saw you through peripheral vision,
Staring at me trying to make a decision.
Please look at my beautiful profile,
It's because of you I can finally smile.
You helped me get my mind right,
You stayed by my side when I was trife,
I never discounted the hustler in you,
I accept you for all that you do.
Your boy told me you make women disappear,
Except for me,
You tried to keep me near.
That's why I remained faithful to you.
You whispered in my ear, it's all for you.
Can't you see what this hustling is doing to me.

For the first time, it's making me want to leave.
Sometimes I wonder if I was full of drama,
Would you respect me, or treat me like your baby's mama.
I refuse to let tears become a part of my heart,
It's a shame only a pen, can flow my thoughts.
So baby, where do I go from here?
Because I refuse to cry another damn tear.

Thank You

I would first like to give thanks to God. I didn't start to heal until I let you into my life.

My father Roy L. Jackson who provided me with all the things a child could ever want.

My best friend Sonya Clark, I will always love you.

Daddy, you took me through my highs and my lows and I don't regret one moment.

Chastity Day, you were one of the few that kept reminding me of my gift.

Mary-Alice Hines, the best psychologist in Atlanta.

Korey, my beautiful son. There are so many things I want to tell you about my life.

Elaine Carter Jones, those phone calls kept me going.

To my loved ones that are gone but not forgotten.

Peggy A Gordon Jackson, Mommy I know you can see my tears from heaven.

Mason Gordon Jr., you were the first face I saw at my graduation, and I love you.

My grandmother Juanita Gordon, I wish I had more time to spend with you.

My grandfather Mason Gordon Sr., I wish we had more time together.

Great Grandma Sally, you will always be a reminder of the old days, and country living.

Special Thanks

Photographer Averi Washington @ Ntheloop.com

And

Ace @ Apace Cafe

God Bless, Rosalind

ISBN 1-41205111-8

9 781412 051118